BORN LUCKY

A Dedicated Father, A Grateful Son,
and My Journey with Autism

Leland Vittert

Don Yaeger

2025. All rights reserved.

No part of this book may be reproduced, stored, or transmitted

in any form or by any means, electronic, mechanical,

photocopying, recording, scanning, or otherwise, except as

permitted under Section 107 or 108 of the 1976 United States

Copyright Act, without the prior written permission of the

Publisher.

@ **LELAND VITTERT**

TABLE OF CONTENT

Born Lucky..0
A Dedicated Father, A Grateful Son, and My Journey with Autism.. 0
Silent Beginnings...8
    First Words and First Silences.................................. 8
    The House My Family Made for Me........................ 8
    Early Signs Parents Didn't Yet Name.......................9
We Didn't Have a Label (Yet)..................................... 11
    Pediatric Visits, Bewildered Teachers, and the Normalizing of Oddness.. 11
    How the School System Handled (and Didn't Handle) Me... 12
Mark — The Father Who Saw a Different Map.......14
    Sketch of My Father's Character and Instincts........14
    The Decision That Would Redefine Our Household... 15
The First Interventions...17
    Early Therapies and the Pragmatic Faith of a Parent.. 17
    Small Wins: Speech, Routines, the First Routines That Stuck... 18
Training a Son — Not the Way You Think.................21
    My Father's Regimen: Practice in Manners, Eye Contact, Humor, Resilience...................................... 21
    Why He Quit His Job and What That Looked Like Day to Day.. 22

Rehearsing Humanity..24
    Role-Playing Social Situations: Interviews, Playground Encounters, Family Dinners.................24
    The Ethics and Love Behind Coaching a Child to "Perform" Social Skill... 25

Lessons That Looked Like Tough Love......................27
    Pushups, Blunt Feedback, Accountability Rituals...27
    When Discipline Helped and When It Bruised........28

I Was the Kid They Did Not Understand................... 31
    Classroom Misunderstandings and Sensory Overload 31
    The Cost of Being Labeled "Weird".........................32

Bullies, Bystanders, and Small Mercy........................ 34
    Specific Episodes of Bullying and How I Learned to Navigate Them..34
    Teachers Who Helped, and Those Who Didn't....... 35

School as Training Ground..37
    Tactical Social Training Applied to the Cafeteria, Assemblies, and Gym Class...................................... 37
    Moments of Success That Felt Like Miracles......... 38

Friendship by Practice... 40
    How Friendships Were Taught, Rehearsed, and Sometimes Genuine...40
    The Distinction Between Learned and Felt Connection..41

Mirrors and Performance — Teenaged Self............. 44
    Self-Consciousness, the Media I Consumed, and Finding Role Models.. 44

    The First Sparks of Wanting a Public Voice............ 45
The First Crush, The First Loss.................................. 47
    Learning Intimacy Under Instruction...................... 47
    Heartbreak and the Awkward Arithmetic of Teenage Feelings... 48
High School Stagecraft... 50
    Debate Team, School Paper, and Other Spaces to Practice Presence... 50
    Early Broadcasting Experiments and the Thrill of Being Heard.. 51
Choosing Journalism — Why the Mic Felt Like a Safe Place... 54
    How Storytelling Made Sense of the World............ 54
    Training, Mentors, and the First Professional Breaks. 55
Interviewing People, Interviewing Myself................. 57
    Translating the Techniques My Father Taught into Journalistic Craft... 57
    The Discipline of Preparation and the Anxiety Behind Live TV... 58
When the Camera Looks Back.................................... 60
    On-Air Mistakes, Sensory Overwhelm, and Learning to Manage Adrenaline... 60
    Tools I Used to Steady Myself Before Every Show 61
Fame, Scrutiny, and the Public Gaze......................... 63
    Navigating Criticism When You Still Have Private Obligations... 63
    How Public Visibility Affected My Family

Dynamics..64
Mark's Sacrifices, Mark's Faith.................................68
    Deep Portrait of My Father: His Doubts, His Humor, His Stubborn Love...68
    Lessons He Taught That Shaped My Moral Compass. 69

Gratitude With Complications.................................. 71
    The Messy Emotions of Indebtedness: Pride, Resentment, Relief..71
    Real Conversations We Had About Debt, Expectation, and Freedom... 72

The Day He Stepped Back... 74
    Transitioning from Coached Son to Independent Adult.. 74
    Father-Son Adjustments and New Boundaries........ 75

Relationships on My Terms...................................... 78

Parenthood (or Choosing Not To) — Decisions After Diagnosis...81
    Fatherhood and What It Taught Me About Legacy. 81
    Decisions About Family, Work, and Life Priorities. 82

The Tools That Stick..84
    Practical Tools I Still Use: Routines, Mindfulness Hacks, Pre-Show Rituals... 84
    How I Take Care of Sensory Needs in a Busy Life. 85

On Labels, Identity, and the Spectrum......................88
    My Views on the Term Autism and What It Has Meant Personally and Culturally............................. 88

Parenting a Child on the Spectrum — Advice I Give

Young Parents **91**
    Concrete, Compassionate Guidance for Parents Who Feel Lost 91
    What I Wish My Parents Had Known and What Worked 92

Systems That Help — Schools, Healthcare, Policy ... 94
    Practical Reforms and Resources That Would Have Made a Difference 94
    Where Institutions Still Fail Families Like Mine 96

When the Story Becomes Public — Media, Misunderstanding, Opportunity 97
    How Public Narratives Shape Perceptions of Autism. 97
    The Responsibility of Storytellers and Journalists .. 98

Early Days: Small Town, Big Questions

SILENT BEGINNINGS

FIRST WORDS AND FIRST SILENCES

The earliest memories do not begin with sound but with its absence. Other children babbled, their voices filling kitchens and playgrounds with nonsense syllables that soon tumbled into words. In my case, the silence lingered like an uninvited guest. My parents waited for the "mama" or "dada" that never came, measuring time not by milestones but by the long stretches of nothing. There were noises — humming, repetitive sounds, fragments that never quite became speech — but the expected bridge into language refused to appear. To them it was unsettling, a reminder that something essential was missing, though neither of them yet had a name for it. For me, those silences were a kind of comfort, a rhythm I understood better than words, though I could not explain that at the time.

THE HOUSE MY FAMILY MADE FOR ME

In the absence of words, my world was built from spaces, objects, and routines. The family home became more than walls; it was a carefully arranged landscape of safety and familiarity. My mother kept the kitchen warm with the smell of bread or soup simmering, as though nourishment could coax me into speaking. My father's presence filled the house with a different kind of energy — protective, expectant, quietly restless. Toys were lined up in precise order across the floor, books stacked in patterns that only I seemed to recognize. The house spoke to me in textures, in the creak of the hallway floorboards, in the way light spilled across the living room in the afternoons. It was less a place of conversation and more a silent theater where my family tried to decode me, each room carrying both their hope and their worry.

Early Signs Parents Didn't Yet Name

Looking back, the signs were there from the beginning, though in those years the language of autism was not as familiar, not as available to ordinary families. My fascination with spinning objects, the way I avoided eye contact, the meltdowns triggered by sudden changes — all of these were signals, but to my parents they were only mysteries. Teachers and relatives suggested I was "shy," "slow to warm up," or perhaps just stubborn. My father began keeping mental notes, trying to detect patterns in my behavior, while my mother clung to reassurances from doctors who insisted that some children simply take longer to talk. Beneath these attempts to normalize, though, both of them sensed the truth pressing at the edges of their understanding. The silence wasn't random. It was the first chapter of a story neither of them had expected to tell.

We Didn't Have a Label (Yet)

Pediatric Visits, Bewildered Teachers, and the Normalizing of Oddness

The first stop on the long road to understanding was always the pediatrician's office. My mother, armed with a mental list of questions, tried to capture what she noticed at home — the silences, the fixations, the awkwardness that didn't fade as quickly as it should have. Doctors nodded politely, flipped through charts, tapped their pens against clipboards. They measured my height and weight, tested my hearing, shone lights into my eyes, but when it came to the quietness that worried her most, they shrugged. Some children, they said, simply bloomed later. The word "late" was repeated so often that it began to sound like reassurance, though it was really an evasion.

Teachers saw something too, though they didn't have the language to frame it. In classrooms buzzing with noise, I sat apart, not unfriendly but unreachable. They noted how I would stare at patterns on the wall instead of raising my hand, or how I melted down when schedules changed. They described me in reports with words like "different," "quirky," or "distractible." None of these terms carried the gravity of a diagnosis, and so my parents were left stitching together half-answers, caught between doctors who promised patience would be enough and teachers who hinted that patience might not be the cure.

How the School System Handled (and Didn't Handle) Me

School was meant to be the place where children found structure, but for me it often felt like a proving ground that magnified everything I struggled with. The system was designed for children who could sit still, follow unwritten rules, and grasp social cues without coaching. I was not that child. Instead, I became the one who disrupted routines by not understanding them, the one who cried at fire drills, the one who refused to line up properly because the noise and jostling overwhelmed me.

Without a formal label, teachers did what they thought best. Some extended extra patience, offering gentle encouragement when I lagged behind, allowing me to fidget or step aside when the classroom became too much. Others were less forgiving, interpreting my differences as disobedience. Notes went home describing behavior problems rather than neurological ones, painting me as a child who simply needed more discipline. My parents read these notes late at night at the kitchen table, frustration mounting as they tried to reconcile two versions of me: the one they loved fiercely at home and the one who baffled educators.

The truth is, without a diagnosis, the system didn't quite know what to do with me. I was neither fully failing nor fully thriving, caught in a gray area where expectations were constantly adjusted but never clearly defined. The normalizing of oddness — as though my quirks were harmless — delayed the search for deeper answers. It kept me in a place where survival was possible, but thriving was not. And for my parents, every parent-teacher conference carried the same undertone: something was wrong, but no one could tell us what.

Mark — The Father Who Saw a Different Map

Sketch of My Father's Character and Instincts

My father was not the kind of man who liked to sit still. He was restless in the way that successful people often are, always moving, always searching for a challenge just beyond the horizon. He had built a career on instinct — trusting his gut, spotting opportunities where others saw problems. Yet at home, those same instincts began to tell him something the professionals would not: his son was on a different path, and the roadmaps handed down by doctors and teachers were not enough to guide him.

Mark was practical, not sentimental, but his practicality was fused with a deep sense of loyalty. He was the sort of man who believed that hard work could solve most problems, and if hard work failed, then more hard work would be the answer. To him, my silences and peculiarities were not barriers to acceptance but puzzles to solve. Where others shrugged or reassured, he took notes. Where others told my parents to wait and see, he pressed forward with questions of his own. My father was not a trained therapist, not a doctor or specialist, but he carried the unshakable belief that he could figure things out if he paid close enough attention.

The Decision That Would Redefine Our Household

The moment of decision did not arrive with fanfare, but its consequences rippled through every part of our lives. My father looked at the uncertain answers coming from the outside world and decided that waiting for a solution was no longer an option. If the system could not provide a map for me, then he would draw one himself. And so he did something most fathers of his generation would never have considered — he stepped away from his work to dedicate himself fully to mine.

It was not framed as a sacrifice, though in many ways it was. It meant financial adjustments, new routines, and a household reordered around a single mission: helping me find a way to navigate a world that did not yet make sense. My father approached it like a coach building a training program. He began designing exercises that others might have dismissed as trivial — practicing eye contact over dinner, rehearsing jokes until the timing landed, enforcing pushups when I avoided uncomfortable situations. To him, these were not punishments but lessons in resilience, drills for a life that would demand more from me than it did from most.

The decision redefined not only our household but also our relationship. He was not simply my father anymore; he was my trainer, my advocate, my sparring partner, my fiercest believer. Every day became a session, every outing a practice run for the larger stage of life. While the world continued to call me different, he chose to see me as untested — a boy who could, with enough guidance, grow into a man capable of facing any room, any conversation, any challenge.

THE FIRST INTERVENTIONS

Early Therapies and the Pragmatic Faith of a Parent

The word *intervention* carries the weight of something clinical, but in our home it began as something improvised, stitched together by love and a parent's determination. My father refused to let my differences be reduced to shrugging reassurances or vague promises that time would fix everything. If language was not arriving on its own, then he would find ways to coax it into existence. He read everything he could, asked questions of therapists, and then transformed those ideas into everyday practice.

Speech therapy was one of the first structured steps. I remember the sterile office with its fluorescent lights, the stack of flashcards, the slow syllables repeated over and over until they blurred together. At first, the exercises felt foreign, like being asked to mimic a tune I could not hear. My father, however, treated each session like a warm-up drill. He sat beside me, repeating the sounds, exaggerating his lips, urging me to try again. He was less concerned with the therapist's report than with the small moments when a new sound slipped past my resistance. To him, every "ma" or "ba" was proof that the door could be pushed open wider, no matter how heavy it seemed.

There were other therapies too, often experimental, some abandoned after a few weeks when it became clear they didn't fit. Yet my father never treated failure as wasted effort. To him, each attempt was part of a larger strategy, a collection of tools that could be tested, adapted, and refined. It was a pragmatic kind of faith — not the blind belief that everything would work out, but the conviction that steady work would eventually yield results.

SMALL WINS: SPEECH, ROUTINES, THE FIRST ROUTINES THAT STUCK

Progress came in fragments, so small at first that outsiders might have dismissed them. A word spoken clearly at the dinner table. A toy put back in the same place two days in a row. A meltdown avoided because I knew what was coming next. These were not grand victories, but in a household that had lived with uncertainty for so long, they were enough to celebrate.

Speech, especially, felt like unlocking a hidden treasure. The first time I strung together a full sentence —

awkward, halting, but unmistakably mine — my father's face carried a mix of relief and triumph, as though he had just watched me cross a finish line no one else believed I could reach. Words became tools, and then bridges. They allowed me to ask, to protest, to connect, even if imperfectly.

Routines became the backbone of stability. My father introduced them like a coach laying out plays before a big game. Mornings followed a script: wake up, get dressed, breakfast, eye contact practice before heading out the door. Evenings had their own rhythm — reading, reflection, and sometimes role-playing social situations I might face the next day. At first I resisted, as children often do, but over time the predictability gave me a sense of control. Within those routines, my confidence began to grow.

Looking back, these early wins were not just about skill-building. They were about shifting the atmosphere of our home from fear to momentum. The silence that once felt like an unscalable wall had begun to crack, and through those cracks my father glimpsed something worth all the effort: possibility.

Diagnosis, Defiance, and the Work of Parenting

TRAINING A SON — NOT THE WAY YOU THINK

My Father's Regimen: Practice in Manners, Eye Contact, Humor, Resilience

Most children learn manners in passing — a reminder at the dinner table, a gentle correction when they forget to say "please" or "thank you." For me, it was drilled like a sport. My father turned the small, invisible rituals of daily life into practice rounds. If I forgot to make eye contact, he stopped me mid-sentence and asked me to start again. If I answered too abruptly, he would coach me on tone, on pacing, on the importance of leaving space in a conversation. To outsiders it might have looked harsh, but for us it was training.

He believed humor was a form of social currency, so he built it into the curriculum. Jokes were tested and retested, timing adjusted, punchlines rephrased until they landed. Resilience, too, was part of the regimen. If I grew frustrated and gave up, he countered with pushups or another physical task. His message was clear: life wouldn't go easier on me because I had autism, so I had to learn how to stay in the game, even when it was hard. Every correction, every drill, every repeated exercise carried the same underlying lesson — I was capable of more, and he would not let me settle for less.

Why He Quit His Job and What That Looked Like Day to Day

The turning point in our family's story was not just the diagnosis but my father's response to it. Most men in his position would have doubled down on work, chasing financial security as a way to care for their family. My father did the opposite. He stepped away from his career, a decision that baffled colleagues and even some relatives, because he believed his most important work was now inside our home.

Day to day, that choice reshaped our lives. Our mornings started earlier, because he insisted that routine was the foundation of discipline. Breakfast was followed not by idle play but by drills: practicing conversation starters, rehearsing classroom interactions, working on posture and tone. Afternoons might involve role-playing how to order food at a restaurant or how to introduce myself to a neighbor. Evenings became a review session, with my father asking what I had learned, where I had struggled, and how I planned to handle tomorrow.

To a child, it sometimes felt relentless, like living inside a never-ending practice field. But underneath the structure was something I did not yet recognize — a father who was determined to equip me with tools that no school, no therapist, no institution seemed willing to provide. He saw a different map for my life, one where autism was not an endpoint but a challenge to be prepared for. His decision to quit his job was not just an act of sacrifice; it was a declaration that my future was worth betting everything on.

REHEARSING HUMANITY

ROLE-PLAYING SOCIAL SITUATIONS: INTERVIEWS, PLAYGROUND ENCOUNTERS, FAMILY DINNERS

In most families, the dinner table is a place for eating and conversation. In ours, it was also a stage. My father turned meals into rehearsals, teaching me how to look someone in the eye as I asked for the salt, how to pause after a joke so others had time to laugh, how to listen without interrupting. He made the ordinary moments of family life into scripted lessons, as though each one were a preview of a larger performance I would someday give in the world outside our walls.

Playground encounters were no different. Before we went to the park, we practiced what I should say if another child asked me to join a game, or how to react if they said no. At first, these scenarios felt artificial, like learning lines for a play. But with repetition they became second nature. By the time I stood on the edge of a kickball game, the words were already waiting on my tongue, rehearsed in the living room a hundred times before.

Even interviews — something most children wouldn't face until much later in life — were part of his training plan. He would sit across from me at the kitchen table, pretending to be a teacher, a camp counselor, or even a future employer. He drilled me on how to answer questions with confidence, how to shake hands firmly, how to project presence even when I felt unsure. It was practice for situations that hadn't yet arrived, but in my father's eyes, preparation was the only way to meet a world that would not bend itself to me.

The Ethics and Love Behind Coaching a Child to "Perform" Social Skill

At times, my training felt less like childhood and more like theater. I was being coached to perform "normal" — to smile when expected, to laugh on cue, to navigate conversations with rules that felt foreign. The question of authenticity lingers when I look back. Was I becoming myself, or simply learning to mask the parts of me that others found uncomfortable?

For my father, the distinction mattered less than the outcome. He believed love required giving me the best chance to stand on equal footing with my peers, even if that meant rehearsing behaviors that did not come naturally. Some might have judged it as forcing a child to hide, but in our home it was framed as empowerment. He wasn't trying to erase who I was; he was trying to give me tools to survive in a world that would not always understand me.

And behind every drill, every correction, every role-play exercise was a current of love. My father's methods were demanding, sometimes exhausting, but they were never detached. He invested himself fully, sitting across from me night after night, repeating lines and gestures until they stuck. What I carried into the world was not just a set of rehearsed social skills but the knowledge that someone believed I was worth the effort — that my future mattered enough to be practiced into being.

LESSONS THAT LOOKED LIKE TOUGH LOVE

PUSHUPS, BLUNT FEEDBACK, ACCOUNTABILITY RITUALS

In our house, discipline didn't always look like a scolding or a punishment. More often, it looked like sweat. If I slipped into laziness, if I resisted the routines my father thought essential, he would tell me to drop and give him pushups. The exercise was not just about physical strength but about training my mind to push through resistance. My arms ached, my chest burned, and yet with each repetition I felt a small part of myself stretch toward resilience. He believed struggle built character, and that a body trained to endure discomfort could carry a mind through the harder battles of life.

Feedback in our house was rarely sugarcoated. My father did not dress criticism in soft words or gentle tones. If I mumbled, he would say, "Speak up. No one can hear you like that." If I avoided eye contact, he would stop me mid-sentence and remind me: "Look at me. People need to see you." His bluntness stung, but it cut through ambiguity. I always knew where I stood with him — no false praise, no empty comfort. In a world where I often misunderstood cues or subtleties, his directness was its own kind of gift.

Accountability was built into daily rituals. At the end of each day, he asked me to review what I had done well and where I had fallen short. It became our version of prayer, a quiet reflection that forced me to measure myself against the standards he set. Some nights it felt empowering; other nights, it felt like failure written into ritual. Still, the habit taught me to see progress and shortcomings not as accidents, but as things I had the power to shape.

WHEN DISCIPLINE HELPED AND WHEN IT BRUISED

Discipline, like any tool, cuts both ways. On my best days, my father's methods instilled in me grit, a sense of self-mastery I would lean on long after childhood. Pushups in the living room became metaphors for pushing through life's disappointments. His no-nonsense feedback toughened my skin against a world that would often be harsher still. In those moments, discipline was love translated into structure, preparing me for realities he knew I would face without him there to shield me.

But there were times when his tough love left bruises that didn't show on skin. The constant demand for improvement could feel like a relentless spotlight, one that left little room for simply being a child. I sometimes mistook his correction for rejection, his intensity for disappointment in who I was rather than what I did. It took me years to separate the methods from the motive, to understand that his sternness was not absence of love but a different language for it.

Looking back, I see both sides. My father's toughness shaped me in ways nothing else could have, yet it also demanded costs I carried quietly. The balance between building resilience and nurturing gentleness is one few parents ever master. In our story, discipline was both the weight that strengthened my muscles and the burden that sometimes pressed too heavily. What remained constant, though, was the certainty that every pushup, every blunt word, every ritual of accountability was tethered to the same unshakable belief: that I was capable of more than I knew, and that it was his job to draw it out of me.

School, Bullying, and the Mechanics of Surviving

I WAS THE KID THEY DID NOT UNDERSTAND

CLASSROOM MISUNDERSTANDINGS AND SENSORY OVERLOAD

School was never just about reading, writing, and arithmetic for me; it was about survival. The classroom, with its buzzing fluorescent lights, the scrape of chairs across tile, the smell of glue and crayons mingling in the air, was a place that demanded a kind of endurance no one else seemed to need. Teachers saw me fidgeting or covering my ears and thought I was distracted, careless, or disrespectful. What they could not see was the storm of sensory information I was battling every moment — every flicker of light, every whisper at the edge of hearing, every shifting smell pulling at me all at once.

Instructions that seemed simple to others often landed in pieces for me. By the time I pieced together the first part of what the teacher said, the rest had already vanished in the air. My hesitations looked like disobedience; my silence looked like indifference. When I blurted out answers or repeated lines from television shows, it wasn't mischief — it was the only way I knew to bridge the gap between myself and the classroom rhythm I could never quite join.

The misunderstandings compounded over time. Notes home painted me as inattentive or disruptive. Teachers spoke of "potential" one moment and "behavior problems" the next. Each misread made the ground under me less stable, convincing me that no matter how hard I tried, school was a game rigged for children built differently than I was.

The Cost of Being Labeled "Weird"

Children are quick to notice difference, and even quicker to name it. On the playground, my pauses, my too-literal responses, my unusual fixations made me stand out. "Weird" was the word that stuck, a single syllable sharp enough to slice through any hope of blending in. It followed me in whispers, in laughter when I missed a joke, in the quiet exclusion from games where I didn't quite fit.

Being labeled "weird" was more than an insult — it was a cage. It told me I was outside the circle before I even had the chance to step in. It stripped away the possibility of being seen for my effort, my curiosity, or my kindness. It meant I walked into classrooms and cafeterias with a shadow already cast over me, one I could never outrun.

The cost of that label was heavy. It wasn't just loneliness; it was the slow erosion of trust in myself. Every sidelong glance, every laugh at my expense made me question whether I was truly capable of belonging anywhere. My father fought to teach me resilience, to remind me that "weird" was not a verdict on my worth. But in the moment, sitting at my desk with the hum of fluorescent lights drilling into my head and the word "weird" echoing in my ears, it felt like a life sentence.

And yet, somewhere beneath the weight of misunderstanding, a quiet truth began to take shape. I was not broken, even if the world had no name yet for what I carried. I was simply living in a reality others couldn't see. That realization, though faint at first, would grow into a strength that no label could take away.

BULLIES, BYSTANDERS, AND SMALL MERCY

SPECIFIC EPISODES OF BULLYING AND HOW I LEARNED TO NAVIGATE THEM

Cruelty in childhood rarely announces itself with grand gestures. It comes in whispers, in sudden laughter when you walk past, in the sting of a nickname repeated until it carves itself into your skin. I remember being cornered by boys twice my size who thought it was funny to mimic the way I spoke or to snatch away my backpack and toss it across the playground like a game of keep-away. The humiliation was sharper than any shove or push. It told me in no uncertain terms that I was an object of amusement, not a peer.

Some days, the bullying was quiet — subtle mockery, rolled eyes, the deliberate exclusion from group projects or lunch tables. Other days, it was loud and physical, leaving me bruised not just on the outside but somewhere deeper, in the part of me that had begun to believe I might never belong. What hurt most was not always the act itself but the chorus of laughter or silence from those who stood nearby. To be mocked was painful, but to be unseen or unprotected made the pain linger long after the bruises faded.

Learning to navigate bullying became a survival skill. My father's voice echoed in my head: *"Stand tall, even when you're shaking inside."* Sometimes I fought back with words rehearsed at home, sharp retorts meant to deflect ridicule. Other times I tried to disappear, retreating into myself until the storm passed. Neither approach was foolproof, but both were attempts at reclaiming a small measure of control in a world where my differences made me a target. Over time, I learned to recognize patterns, to spot the warning signs before the ridicule began, and to carve out spaces where I could breathe without fear of attack.

Teachers Who Helped, and Those Who Didn't

Adults were not immune to the role of bystander. Some teachers turned their heads, too busy or too uncertain to intervene. Their silence, whether born of indifference or helplessness, made the classroom feel less like a place of learning and more like a stage where cruelty was tolerated as part of the curriculum. Each ignored episode confirmed to my classmates that their behavior was permissible, that "boys will be boys" or "kids will be kids" was enough to excuse the harm being done.

But there were also teachers who saw me — really saw me. One let me eat lunch in the quiet of her classroom when the cafeteria became too overwhelming. Another pulled me aside after class, not to scold but to listen, to ask how I was doing in a way that suggested she truly wanted to know. These small mercies were lifelines. They didn't erase the cruelty, but they reminded me that kindness existed alongside it, that not every adult was blind to the struggles I faced.

The contrast between those who helped and those who didn't left a lasting mark. I learned that authority did not guarantee protection, that some people would always choose convenience over compassion. Yet I also learned to treasure the rare souls who stepped in, however quietly, to ease the weight I carried. Their actions, modest as they might have seemed, told me I was worth protecting. And in a childhood where the label "weird" so often defined me, those moments of recognition were a form of salvation.

SCHOOL AS TRAINING GROUND

Tactical Social Training Applied to the Cafeteria, Assemblies, and Gym Class

For most kids, school was just school — a place of tests and homework, friendships and games. For me, it was a proving ground, where the lessons my father drilled into me at home were tested in the wild. The cafeteria, in particular, was a battlefield. The noise, the crowded tables, the unspoken politics of who sat where — it was overwhelming. Yet my father had prepared me. We had rehearsed how to ask, *"Mind if I sit here?"* We practiced how to hold a tray without looking clumsy, how to join a conversation with a comment instead of barging in. It felt scripted, but in that loud, chaotic room, the scripts gave me something solid to hold on to.

Assemblies were another test. Sitting still among hundreds of restless students, trying not to flinch at the feedback from the microphone or the echo of clapping, was a kind of endurance I had to build slowly. My father had taught me tricks: deep breaths, fixing my eyes on one steady point, breaking the overwhelming moment into smaller, more manageable pieces. To anyone else, I might have looked quiet, maybe even bored, but inside I was running through the techniques we had practiced like a soldier repeating drills under fire.

Gym class posed its own challenges. Team sports required instincts I didn't naturally have — the rhythm of a game, the flow of unspoken signals between players. I lagged, hesitated, missed cues. But my father had taught me how to compensate: watch for patterns, predict movements, treat the game like a puzzle rather than chaos. I was never the star athlete, but I began to survive gym class without the same constant humiliation that once defined it. Each survival was a victory, proof that the training at home could be carried into the unpredictable terrain of school life.

Moments of Success That Felt Like Miracles

Every so often, the drills paid off not just in survival but in something that felt almost like belonging. The first time I made a joke in the cafeteria and heard laughter that wasn't at my expense, it felt like lightning striking. For once, I wasn't the odd one out; I was part of the current. I carried that moment with me for days, replaying it in my head as evidence that I could, even briefly, touch the world others lived in so easily.

In gym class, I remember catching a ball cleanly — not fumbling, not dropping it — and hearing teammates cheer. It was a small play in a game that meant little in the long run, but for me, it was transformative. For the first time, I wasn't the liability to be hidden at the far edge of the field. For one shining second, I was part of the team.

Even assemblies, where silence was demanded and discomfort was constant, offered small miracles. I remember being asked to help set up chairs once, a responsibility no one expected me to manage smoothly. But I did it — quietly, efficiently, without drawing negative attention. The teacher's nod of approval felt enormous, a confirmation that I wasn't always the kid who got it wrong.

These moments didn't erase the difficulties. They didn't make the cafeteria quiet, the assemblies less overwhelming, or the gym less intimidating. But they were proof that training and persistence could carve out pockets of success in hostile terrain. To anyone else, they might have looked ordinary. To me, they were miracles — fragile, fleeting, but powerful enough to keep me trying again the next day.

FRIENDSHIP BY PRACTICE

How Friendships Were Taught, Rehearsed, and Sometimes Genuine

For many children, friendship grows naturally, like grass between cracks in the sidewalk. For me, it was planted, watered, and carefully tended under my father's watchful eye. He treated friendship like another skill to be taught, broken into steps and practiced until they became second nature. We rehearsed how to greet someone, how to ask a question that showed interest, how to share without making it all about myself. He explained the invisible rules — that a friend doesn't always want to hear your favorite fact for the tenth time, that sometimes it's better to listen than to talk.

Our living room became a stage where I acted out conversations with imaginary classmates, guided by my father's corrections. "Try again," he'd say when I turned the subject back to myself too quickly. "Wait for their answer," he'd remind me when I rushed through a question. Slowly, the rehearsals began to bleed into real life. At recess, I would stand at the edge of a group and summon the courage to use one of our practiced lines. Sometimes it worked. A child would let me in, and for a few minutes, the script carried me along. Other times, it fell flat, and I was left standing outside the circle once again.

And yet, there were moments when practice opened the door to something real. One boy liked the same cartoon I did, and suddenly the lines I had rehearsed weren't just exercises but an entry into shared excitement. Another girl laughed at a joke I had practiced with my father, and then laughed again when I tried a new one on my own. Those were the cracks where something genuine sprouted, fragile but alive.

The Distinction Between Learned and Felt Connection

The friendships born out of practice always carried a certain uncertainty. I could never be sure if the connection was real or just the result of my careful training. Was this classmate sitting with me at lunch because they liked me, or because I had mastered the right balance of listening and talking? Was their smile directed at me, or at the version of myself my father had carefully taught me to perform?

At times, the distinction weighed heavily. Learned connection felt like wearing a costume that fit well enough to pass but never quite felt like my own skin. Felt connection — the rare moments when someone laughed with me, not at me, or when a classmate sought me out instead of the other way around — was like sunlight breaking through clouds. It was rare, unpredictable, and beyond rehearsal.

Looking back, I see that both kinds of connection mattered. The learned friendships, even if fragile, gave me access to experiences I might otherwise have missed. They let me sit at the lunch table, join the game, share in the noise of childhood life. The felt friendships, however rare, gave me something deeper — proof that I could be accepted not just for the skills I had been taught but for the person I was beneath them.

My father's methods built the bridge, but it was those fleeting moments of authenticity that gave me the courage to keep crossing it. In a world where I was so often misunderstood, even one genuine friend felt like a miracle.

Teen Years: Identity and Ambition

Mirrors and Performance — Teenaged Self

Self-Consciousness, the Media I Consumed, and Finding Role Models

Adolescence sharpened the mirror I held up to myself. Where once I stumbled through childhood unaware of how much I stood apart, as a teenager I became acutely conscious of every difference. I noticed how others dressed, how easily they joked, how seamlessly they moved through hallways and conversations. I, on the other hand, rehearsed every gesture, measuring myself against an imagined audience even when no one was watching. The mirror was rarely kind, reflecting a version of me that always seemed one step behind.

Media became my classroom. Television shows, movies, and even news anchors offered me templates of how to speak, how to hold myself, how to react with timing that felt just out of reach in real life. I studied actors the way some kids studied athletes, breaking down their body language, their rhythm of speech, the way their faces shifted to match emotion. Sitcoms taught me the shape of banter. Films showed me how heroes carried themselves. News broadcasts introduced me to voices that commanded attention without raising volume. Each screen was a window, but also a guidebook.

Role models began to take shape out of these flickering images. Some were celebrities who embodied charisma I could only dream of, while others were quieter figures — journalists, writers, thinkers — who seemed to carve space in the world with their words. They became my distant teachers, shaping my sense of who I might become if I could master the same presence. My father's training gave me the mechanics; the media I consumed gave me aspiration.

The First Sparks of Wanting a Public Voice

Until then, survival had been my primary goal — fitting in, not standing out. But somewhere in my teenage years, that shifted. Watching the people I admired, I began to feel the pull of wanting a voice of my own, not just to echo scripts but to speak from something deeper inside me. The idea of having a platform, of being heard rather than tolerated, flickered into possibility.

It began small — a class presentation where I managed to hold attention without stumbling, a debate in which I surprised myself by speaking with clarity. The rush of being listened to, of holding a room for even a few moments, was unlike anything I had rehearsed. It was both terrifying and exhilarating, a glimpse of what it might mean to step beyond performance and into presence.

Of course, insecurity shadowed every spark. Was I truly being heard, or simply playing a role well enough to trick people? Did I deserve attention, or was I borrowing lines from others and passing them off as my own? The questions lingered, but they did not erase the fire that had begun to kindle. For the first time, I imagined a future where my difference was not only something to manage but something that could fuel a voice others might actually want to hear.

Looking back, those teenage years were a rehearsal of a different kind. Not just for social survival, but for identity. The mirror showed me flaws, but it also hinted at potential. The performances I studied became scaffolding for a self that was still under construction. And the first sparks of wanting a public voice marked a turning point: I was no longer content to simply blend into the world. I wanted, cautiously and imperfectly, to speak to it.

THE FIRST CRUSH, THE FIRST LOSS

LEARNING INTIMACY UNDER INSTRUCTION

If friendship had to be taught in steps, then intimacy was a language even more foreign. My father, ever the coach, recognized early on that I would not stumble into romance the way most teenagers did. He sat me down and explained things others took for granted — how to notice someone's interest without misreading every smile, how to compliment without sounding rehearsed, how to respect boundaries even when my own emotions felt overwhelming. It was awkward, even embarrassing, but also necessary. Where other boys seemed to improvise their way through flirting and first dates, I needed scripts, strategies, and a safe place to practice.

My first crush arrived like a lightning strike — sudden, disorienting, impossible to ignore. Every glance from her became magnified, every word replayed in my head long after it was spoken. I relied heavily on the lines my father had drilled into me: ask about her day, listen more than you talk, smile without forcing it. Yet beneath the practice was a current of genuine feeling, something raw and uncoached. For the first time, I wasn't just rehearsing connection — I was aching for it.

Heartbreak and the Awkward Arithmetic of Teenage Feelings

But love, even the clumsy teenage kind, does not follow a script. The girl I liked laughed with me, shared moments that felt electric, and then one day shifted her attention elsewhere, as teenagers do. For her, it may have been a fleeting crush, a passing season. For me, it was a collapse. My father's instruction had prepared me for rejection in theory — *"It won't always work out. You move on."* — but the reality was a math I could not solve. How could something that felt so consuming to me be so casual for her?

The heartbreak was not dramatic in the way movies portray it. There were no tearful goodbyes, no cinematic closure. It was quieter, more humiliating — sitting alone at lunch when she chose another table, hearing her laugh at someone else's joke, realizing the chapter I thought we were writing together had ended without my consent. I felt foolish for believing so deeply, exposed for caring more than the situation deserved.

In time, I learned that this imbalance — the awkward arithmetic of teenage feelings — was part of growing up. My crush had been both real and exaggerated, both practice and pain. The loss stung, but it also revealed something important: that I was capable of longing, of connection, of being moved by someone outside my carefully constructed routines. Even in heartbreak, there was proof that I wasn't only performing life — I was living it, with all its clumsy, tender mess.

Looking back, that first crush and its inevitable loss were less about romance and more about discovery. I learned that intimacy could not always be taught, that feelings could not be rehearsed into neat outcomes. And though the pain felt outsized at the time, it was also the first glimpse of a truth that would follow me into adulthood: love is never simple, and for someone like me, it would always carry both the risk of being misunderstood and the possibility of being fully, beautifully seen.

HIGH SCHOOL STAGECRAFT

DEBATE TEAM, SCHOOL PAPER, AND OTHER SPACES TO PRACTICE PRESENCE

By the time I entered high school, I had begun to realize that life gave me very few natural stages where my oddness could be recast as something else — confidence, intellect, even talent. The debate team was one of those places. What might have seemed like an arena of rapid-fire arguments and quick retorts became, for me, a structured battlefield where rules and preparation could outweigh raw instinct. The formality of it was comforting. There was a clear turn to speak, a time to sit, and points to be scored if you followed the structure. I could rehearse for this. I could thrive in this.

The school paper was another unlikely refuge. Writing allowed me to think slowly, to shape my words without the panic of face-to-face conversation. On the page, no one saw the pauses, the stumbles, the moments when my mind scrambled for footing. Editors appreciated my persistence, my way of noticing details others overlooked. For once, my need to analyze every angle was not seen as obsessive — it was called thorough, even professional.

In both of these spaces, I began to experiment with a strange new feeling: presence. Not the kind that came naturally to charismatic classmates who could light up a room with a joke or a grin, but a presence that came from preparation, from the quiet satisfaction of stepping into a role I had practiced again and again until it fit.

EARLY BROADCASTING EXPERIMENTS AND THE THRILL OF BEING HEARD

It was around this time that I first discovered broadcasting — small, unofficial experiments with a borrowed microphone, a makeshift setup, and an audience that rarely stretched beyond family and a few patient friends. To most, it might have seemed trivial, even nerdy, but for me it was intoxicating. Speaking into that mic gave me a way to shape my voice, to send words out into the world without having to manage the tangle of facial expressions, gestures, and eye contact that had always been such heavy baggage.

There was a thrill in it, not just in hearing my own voice amplified but in the possibility that someone, somewhere, might actually be listening. It felt like a kind of shortcut — a way to bypass the barriers of social awkwardness and step directly into the flow of communication. For a boy who often felt invisible in hallways and classrooms, the idea that my voice could carry beyond the walls was liberating.

High school was far from easy. I still bore the label of "different," still navigated the cruel hierarchies of adolescence. But in debate rounds, in articles signed with my byline, and in the crackling feedback of early broadcasts, I found proof that I could be more than the sum of my struggles. Each stage — literal or improvised — was a rehearsal for something larger, a way of teaching myself that presence could be practiced, that being heard was not only possible but deeply, addictively rewarding.

From Local Anchor to National Screens

CHOOSING JOURNALISM — WHY THE MIC FELT LIKE A SAFE PLACE

How Storytelling Made Sense of the World

For most people, journalism is about chasing facts, catching stories before they disappear, and presenting them to the public with authority. For me, it was something deeper, something more instinctual. Storytelling became the architecture that helped me organize a confusing, often overwhelming world. Life had always felt like too much information pouring in at once — the noise of a crowded hallway, the shifting tones of voices, the unspoken rules that everyone else seemed to follow without instruction. Journalism gave me a way to tame that chaos. If I could ask questions, take notes, and shape what I learned into a narrative, suddenly there was order where before there had only been noise.

The microphone felt like a kind of shield. Behind it, I did not have to improvise small talk or decode social cues in real time. Instead, I could focus on the rhythm of my words, the clarity of my story, and the satisfaction of connecting dots others might miss. The mic did not care if I avoided eye contact. The mic did not ask me to smile at the right moments. It simply carried my voice outward, amplifying thought into something others could hear and, at times, even respect.

Training, Mentors, and the First Professional Breaks

College became the proving ground. I gravitated toward campus radio and the student newspaper, places where passion was the only entry ticket. My hours were filled with late-night editing sessions, half-broken recording equipment, and the camaraderie of other students who were just as obsessed with the craft. These were not the high school hallways of whispered judgments — here, the quirks that once made me "different" were suddenly tools. My fixation on details turned into reliable reporting. My tendency to rehearse interactions became preparation for interviews. What had once marked me as odd now gave me an edge.

Mentorship played an enormous role. Professors who noticed my persistence took time to sharpen my instincts, pushing me to think beyond the script and trust my instincts as a storyteller. Older students showed me how to chase leads, to be persistent without being reckless, and to survive rejection without crumbling. With each small assignment — covering a student council debate, narrating a local sports event, interviewing a guest lecturer — I was practicing not just journalism but selfhood.

The first professional breaks came almost by accident. A piece I had written for the campus paper caught the eye of a local editor who needed stringers. An internship opened doors into newsrooms where the chaos was constant but familiar in its own way. I found that I could thrive in environments where others felt overwhelmed because I had been living with overwhelm all my life. Journalism did not erase my challenges, but it gave them purpose.

Choosing journalism was never just about a career. It was about survival. It was about finding a place where my way of seeing the world was not only valid but valuable. The mic, the pen, the story — they were not tools of escape but bridges. They allowed me to step into the world on my own terms, turning what once set me apart into the very thing that defined my path forward.

INTERVIEWING PEOPLE, INTERVIEWING MYSELF

Translating the Techniques My Father Taught into Journalistic Craft

Long before I ever sat across from a politician, a grieving family, or a war survivor, I had already been through hundreds of "interviews" without realizing it. My father had made them a part of my training. At our kitchen table, he would throw questions at me — some simple, some deliberately uncomfortable — and then correct the way I answered. Did I meet his eyes? Did my voice carry conviction? Did I answer directly, or did I get lost in a maze of half-formed thoughts? What he called "life training" became, in retrospect, my first journalism school.

When I finally stepped into the professional world, I realized that much of interviewing was not about clever questions or catching someone off guard. It was about listening, about staying present in a way that gave the other person enough room to reveal themselves. My father's relentless drills had given me something invaluable: the ability to keep focus under pressure, to structure a conversation instead of being swept away by it. What once felt like harsh lessons at home became the scaffolding of my career.

THE DISCIPLINE OF PREPARATION AND THE ANXIETY BEHIND LIVE TV

Preparation became my armor. Before every interview, I would research until the details blurred together, filling notebooks with questions, facts, and follow-ups. The more I knew, the less I feared. It was a defense mechanism against the chaos that live television inevitably brought. The unpredictability of human speech, the technical glitches, the audience watching in real time — all of it could paralyze me if I wasn't ready. So I made preparation into a ritual.

And yet, no amount of preparation could erase the anxiety. Live TV was a peculiar kind of battlefield. There was no pause button, no second draft, no chance to quietly regroup. Every stumble was public, every hesitation magnified. The red light on the camera felt like an unblinking eye, daring me to falter. Sometimes, I did. But other times, to my surprise, I found myself steadier than I expected — not because I was naturally confident, but because I had practiced being uncomfortable for years.

In many ways, every interview was also a mirror. As I asked others about their choices, their fears, their turning points, I found myself reflecting on my own. Their answers tested not only my professionalism but also my empathy, my capacity to inhabit someone else's story without losing my own. Interviewing people meant, inevitably, interviewing myself. Each conversation pushed me to refine not only my craft but my identity — as a journalist, yes, but also as a person who had once been the awkward boy rehearsing human interaction at his father's table.

When the Camera Looks Back

On-Air Mistakes, Sensory Overwhelm, and Learning to Manage Adrenaline

The first time I saw my own image staring back at me on a studio monitor, I froze. It was disorienting — not just because I had to speak while seeing myself, but because I was suddenly aware of every quirk and flaw I had spent years trying to control. The way my hands fidgeted, the way my eyes darted, the way my voice wavered when my nerves surged. It felt less like performing and more like being interrogated by my own reflection.

Mistakes on-air are merciless. In a classroom, you can stumble and recover with little more than a few chuckles from your peers. On television, a missed word, a jumbled statistic, or a pause too long is preserved, replayed, and sometimes mocked. For someone already sensitive to sound, light, and social pressure, the studio was a sensory minefield. The glare of the lights, the hum of equipment, the constant chatter in my earpiece — it all collided at once. I learned to recognize the rush of adrenaline not as an enemy but as a wave I had to surf. Panic meant drowning; focus meant balance.

The hardest part was forgiving myself in public. Viewers rarely saw the hours of preparation, only the slip. Every mistake carried the sting of exposure. Yet over time, I realized that imperfection was part of the job — not something to fear, but something to manage, to absorb, to move through.

Tools I Used to Steady Myself Before Every Show

I began to build rituals. Some were simple, almost invisible. A certain breathing pattern, counting quietly to four on each inhale and exhale, helped slow the racing pulse. I practiced grounding techniques — feeling my shoes press against the floor, noticing the weight of a pen in my hand — anything that anchored me when my senses threatened to scatter.

Preparation remained my anchor, but it took on a new dimension. I stopped aiming for perfect scripts and instead rehearsed recoveries — how to reset after a slip, how to improvise when technology failed, how to redirect a guest who went off track. This shift was liberating. Instead of chasing flawlessness, I trained myself to bend without breaking.

There were also talismans of a sort. A note from my father, tucked into the back of a notebook, reminding me: *"You've already done harder things."* A quiet ritual of tapping my fingers together before going live, something only I knew, a small signal to myself that I was ready.

In time, I stopped seeing the camera as a predator and began to see it as a mirror — not one that accused, but one that reflected the discipline, resilience, and humanity I had fought to cultivate. When the camera looked back, I no longer flinched. I looked right at it and spoke.

FAME, SCRUTINY, AND THE PUBLIC GAZE

NAVIGATING CRITICISM WHEN YOU STILL HAVE PRIVATE OBLIGATIONS

Fame, if that's what you want to call it, never arrived in a single moment. It crept in quietly — the first time someone recognized me at an airport, the unexpected email from a stranger dissecting my delivery, the comments that arrived in real time after every broadcast. At first, it was flattering. Then, quickly, it became exhausting. To live in the public eye meant that every gesture, every word, and even every silence could be judged by someone who didn't know me beyond the screen.

For someone who had spent a lifetime rehearsing humanity, that kind of scrutiny was more than uncomfortable; it was destabilizing. I had been trained to manage conversation, to rehearse eye contact, to control tone. But how could I possibly manage thousands of unseen eyes, each carrying its own expectations and criticisms? The audience was not a person I could anticipate or rehearse for. It was an unpredictable tide.

At the same time, there was the private life that still demanded attention. My family needed me to be present, grounded, and human — not the polished figure on the screen. That tension was the hardest part. To the world, I was confident, collected, and professional. At home, I was still someone's son, someone's brother, navigating old rhythms that had nothing to do with ratings or headlines. Balancing those worlds required a kind of mental double vision: the ability to absorb the glare of public attention while still protecting the fragile spaces of private life.

How Public Visibility Affected My Family Dynamics

Fame magnified everything. Compliments about my work made my family proud, but criticism often cut them deeper than it cut me. They carried the burden of watching someone they loved turned into a caricature by strangers. My father, who had once been my fiercest trainer, now became my fiercest defender. He bristled at unfair critiques, sometimes more than I did. To him, every public attack was not just about my work — it was an assault on the years of discipline and sacrifice that had brought me to that point.

There were also new distances created by visibility. Some relatives hesitated to share private struggles, fearing they might end up as anecdotes in a story or interview. Friends treated me differently, unsure whether they were speaking to the boy they had always known or the journalist they saw on television. Even within the family, my schedule and public obligations often meant missing milestones, dinners, or moments that could never be replayed.

Yet visibility also gave me new responsibilities. People reached out with their own stories — of autism, of parenting, of survival — as if my own journey gave them permission to speak. My family and I had to learn how to hold those stories without being crushed by them. It was a reminder that the public gaze is not just about scrutiny; it can also be about connection. But that connection came at a cost, one that my family paid alongside me.

Living under the gaze of fame required constant recalibration. I was always balancing the external performance with the internal life, always guarding against the danger of letting one eclipse the other. For all the noise of public opinion, the quiet truth remained: I was not just a journalist or a public figure. I was still a son shaped by a father's discipline, a brother bound by family ties, and a man learning, day by day, to live authentically under a light that never went out.

Father and Son: The Long Conversation

MARK'S SACRIFICES, MARK'S FAITH

Deep Portrait of My Father: His Doubts, His Humor, His Stubborn Love

To understand my story, you have to understand my father, Mark. He was not a saint, not a man without temper or flaw, but someone whose stubborn devotion often outweighed his uncertainty. He doubted himself more often than I realized at the time. There were nights when he must have wondered if he had chosen the right path, if quitting his career to focus on me was too reckless, too costly. Yet he rarely showed those doubts openly. Instead, he masked them with humor, with sharp one-liners and the kind of dry wit that made even the hardest lessons sting a little less.

What set him apart was not just the sacrifices he made but the way he made them. He did not retreat into quiet martyrdom; he pressed forward with a stubborn kind of love that refused to accept defeat. His love was not always gentle. It was corrective, sometimes harsh, but it was consistent. And in consistency, I found security. Even when I resented him, even when I argued or balked at his endless drills, I knew he would not walk away.

Lessons He Taught That Shaped My Moral Compass

The lessons my father taught me went beyond eye contact and conversation. They were moral lessons, stitched into the fabric of my daily training. He taught me that words matter, that promises must be kept, that discipline is not punishment but a way of honoring your own potential. When I cut corners, he reminded me that shortcuts leave scars. When I faltered, he insisted that resilience was not about avoiding failure but about returning to your feet after it.

Perhaps his greatest gift was showing me the value of accountability. He held me responsible for my actions long before the world would. That accountability often felt unforgiving in the moment, but it became the backbone of my integrity. He also taught me that humor could coexist with hardship. He could take a situation that felt unbearable and puncture it with a joke that carried us both through.

My father's faith was not just religious, though it carried echoes of that, too. It was a faith in me — in my ability to rise to challenges, to grow into someone who could carry himself in the world. At times, I felt crushed by the weight of that faith, but in truth, it steadied me. It told me that someone had already bet everything on my future, and my task was not to prove him wrong.

When I look at the person I became, I see my father's fingerprints everywhere — in my discipline, my stubbornness, my willingness to stand in the glare of a camera and keep speaking. His sacrifices carved the path I walk, and his faith lit the way.

GRATITUDE WITH COMPLICATIONS

The Messy Emotions of Indebtedness: Pride, Resentment, Relief

Gratitude is rarely simple. On the surface, I knew I owed my father everything. His sacrifices had given me the scaffolding I needed to build a life — not just survival, but achievement, independence, even a career that demanded presence. Pride in him was natural, almost instinctive. I admired the courage it took to turn down a conventional path, to take on the risk of pouring himself so completely into my future.

But along with pride came the more complicated feelings that gratitude often hides. Resentment flared in quiet ways — in the sense that I had not chosen this intensity of instruction, that his sacrifices sometimes cast a shadow too long for me to step out of. Relief was tangled into it as well: relief that I had been seen, trained, carried, when so many others in my position were left to stumble alone. Relief that the weight had not crushed him, and by extension, had not crushed me. Gratitude, then, became a braid of emotions — noble in parts, but also knotted with tension.

REAL CONVERSATIONS WE HAD ABOUT DEBT, EXPECTATION, AND FREEDOM

These feelings eventually had to be spoken aloud. We did not circle around them forever; my father was too direct for that. At different points in my adulthood, we had conversations that cut straight to the heart of it. I asked him, sometimes with anger, sometimes with exhaustion, if he regretted giving up so much for me. His answer was consistent, almost defiant: *"I made a choice. Don't make it a debt."*

He wanted me to live freely, not chained to an eternal obligation to repay him. And yet, freedom from that debt was easier said than felt. The very act of my success — every broadcast, every recognition — felt like a silent acknowledgment of his labor. I wrestled with the paradox: how do you live as your own person when your foundation was laid entirely by another?

We also talked about expectation. He admitted, with a rare crack in his armor, that he sometimes wondered if he had been too hard on me, if he had pushed in ways that might have bruised as much as they built. Hearing that softened me. It reminded me that his love had never been mechanical. It was full of doubt, and yet it carried forward anyway.

Freedom, we decided, lay not in pretending the debt didn't exist, but in redefining it. Not as something I owed him, but as something I carried forward — into the way I worked, the way I treated others, the way I lived my life. Gratitude with complications is still gratitude. It is gratitude that admits its shadows, but chooses, again and again, to stand in the light.

THE DAY HE STEPPED BACK

TRANSITIONING FROM COACHED SON TO INDEPENDENT ADULT

There was no ceremony, no clear announcement, no final drill. But there was a day when I felt it: my father stepping back. For years, he had been the coach, the strategist, the watchful eye that corrected and guided. He monitored my gestures, rehearsed my conversations, sharpened my instincts. His presence was constant, and in its constancy I found both security and pressure. Then, almost imperceptibly, he loosened his grip.

The transition was not sudden — it was gradual, like training wheels coming off. He started by letting me walk into interviews on my own, no last-minute rehearsal. He resisted the urge to critique every broadcast, offering instead the occasional nod or simple, "You did fine." At first, the quiet unnerved me. Silence from him had always meant correction was coming. Now it meant trust. I realized that independence is not given in a single moment; it is allowed, step by step, by someone who loves you enough to stop holding on.

Father-Son Adjustments and New Boundaries

Adjusting to this shift was not easy for either of us. For me, it meant shouldering responsibility without the safety net of constant coaching. Mistakes were mine alone, not part of a joint project. Successes, too, felt different — less like victories shared with him and more like steps I had to own fully. I began to see myself less as a product of his training and more as an adult navigating the world in my own right. That was liberating, but also terrifying.

For my father, stepping back was its own kind of discipline. His identity had been tied to my progress for so long that letting go was, in a sense, a test of his own faith. We had conversations that revealed his struggle. He admitted it was hard to watch me stumble without stepping in, hard to resist the urge to polish every rough edge. Yet he also recognized that clinging too tightly would keep me tethered to a childhood that had long since ended.

We built new boundaries, sometimes awkwardly. Our relationship shifted from coach and trainee to something more even, though the echoes of those old roles never fully disappeared. He remained my father, still stubborn, still protective, but now he allowed space for me to push back, to choose differently, even to fail without him rushing to pick up the pieces.

That day — or rather, that season — when he stepped back was not an ending but a transformation. It marked the beginning of adulthood not defined by constant rehearsal, but by trust. And though the adjustment carried its bumps and silences, it also carried the gift of freedom — freedom earned through years of work, and freedom granted by a father who finally knew he could let go.

Love, Marriage, and Building an Adult Life

RELATIONSHIPS ON MY TERMS

Dating While Practicing Social Scripts and Learning Authenticity

When I first stepped into the world of dating, I carried with me the same toolkit that had helped me navigate classrooms and television studios: rehearsed lines, memorized gestures, and an inner dialogue that ran like a teleprompter. I relied on scripts — not because I wanted to be insincere, but because I didn't yet trust that my natural instincts would be enough. A compliment would be practiced, a question carefully framed, and silence filled with pre-prepared small talk. To many, dating is a dance guided by intuition. For me, it was choreography I had to study and rehearse.

At first, this made relationships feel both exciting and exhausting. Exciting, because I was entering a world of connection and affection I had long imagined. Exhausting, because I often left an evening replaying every word, every glance, every pause, analyzing whether I had missed a cue. I wondered constantly if the other person could sense my calculation. Yet with time, I began to see that authenticity didn't mean abandoning my scripts altogether. It meant using them as scaffolding until I could trust myself to improvise.

What Intimacy Looks Like When You Must Learn to Read Cues

Intimacy, for me, was not something that unfolded effortlessly. It was something I had to study — not in a cold, clinical way, but with the curiosity of someone who knew connection was worth the effort. I learned to notice tone of voice, body language, and pauses not just as signals to decode, but as invitations to be present. I realized that intimacy wasn't about perfection. It was about patience, laughter when I stumbled, and finding people willing to meet me halfway.

There were moments of deep tenderness when all the analysis fell away and I could simply be. Those moments taught me that intimacy isn't a puzzle to be solved, but a practice of trust. Trust in myself, trust in the other person, and trust that even if I misunderstood, the relationship could hold space for correction and growth.

Dating on my terms meant refusing to conform to expectations that didn't fit me. I wasn't the smooth talker or the effortless charmer. I was the thoughtful listener, the person who remembered details others might miss, the one who wanted connection to be real, not performed. Over time, I learned that what some might call awkwardness could also be seen as sincerity.

Relationships became not just about learning others, but about allowing myself to be learned — to be known, in all my quirks and rhythms. That was intimacy on my terms: less about flawless execution, more about honest presence. And in that, I found something far richer than the scripts I once relied on.

PARENTHOOD (OR CHOOSING NOT TO) – DECISIONS AFTER DIAGNOSIS

Fatherhood and What It Taught Me About Legacy

The question of parenthood has always been more than just personal for me; it has been tethered to the story of my diagnosis and the way I was raised. My father poured his entire being into shaping me, not with the usual parental gestures of advice and encouragement, but with daily coaching, relentless attention, and sacrifices that cost him his career. To imagine being a father myself meant reckoning with that model. Could I be that selfless? Would my children inherit some of the struggles I carry?

When I thought about fatherhood, I often pictured my dad leaning over the dinner table, running a drill on eye contact, or standing on the sidelines of life like a tireless coach. The thought was daunting, not because I doubted my love, but because I knew the cost. Raising a child is demanding for any parent. Raising one when you carry both the knowledge of autism and the lived memory of being its student raises the stakes.

If I were to become a father, I would want my legacy to be different: less about constant training and more about balance, joy, and freedom to fail. My dad gave me the tools I needed to stand in the world; my legacy, I hope, would be to give a child the space to breathe in it.

DECISIONS ABOUT FAMILY, WORK, AND LIFE PRIORITIES

For those of us who live with autism, or any difference that requires daily navigation, the decision to have children is not automatic. It involves weighing energy, emotional reserves, and the pull of other priorities. For me, work became both a mission and a sanctuary. Journalism demanded long hours, unpredictable schedules, and the kind of emotional bandwidth that often left little room for anything else. In some ways, my career became my child: it grew because I fed it, disciplined it, and stayed committed when others might have walked away.

The decision not to start a family — at least not yet — was not a rejection of love or intimacy. It was a recognition of capacity. I knew what it meant to give everything, because I had seen my father do it. To step into parenthood casually, without that level of readiness, would have felt dishonest.

Still, the idea of legacy never leaves me. Whether or not I raise a child, I carry the responsibility to pass something forward: resilience, honesty, or perhaps simply the story of how one family navigated autism with love and grit. Parenthood is one form of legacy. But so is the choice to live authentically, to tell my story, and to allow others to learn from it.

In the end, the decision about family is inseparable from the life I've built with and around autism. It is a decision made not out of fear, but out of clarity — about what I can give, and what I must honor in myself.

THE TOOLS THAT STICK

PRACTICAL TOOLS I STILL USE: ROUTINES, MINDFULNESS HACKS, PRE-SHOW RITUALS

The strategies my father drilled into me and the ones I later adapted for myself didn't fade away with childhood. They became the scaffolding of my adult life. Routines, once painstakingly rehearsed, are now second nature. I still wake up and walk through a sequence of steps that bring order before the day brings chaos — coffee measured the same way, headlines scanned in the same order, wardrobe chosen with as little decision-making as possible. Consistency isn't just comfort; it's efficiency.

Mindfulness, for me, isn't about sitting cross-legged in silence. It's about micro-adjustments that help me stay present. Deep breaths before the red light on the camera turns on. A grounding gesture — pressing my thumb and forefinger together — when I feel myself slipping into overwhelm. Even the small act of mentally rehearsing gratitude before a segment goes live centers me. These aren't exotic practices; they're practical hacks, carried like tools in my pocket.

Pre-show rituals, too, are my anchor. A written outline I never fully rely on but always prepare. A sip of water taken deliberately. A brief moment of stillness behind the set, as if I'm shaking hands with my nerves before asking them to step aside. What looks like calm on screen is often a choreography of invisible tools keeping me steady.

How I Take Care of Sensory Needs in a Busy Life

Busy public life doesn't erase the fact that sensory overload can still ambush me. The difference is that I've learned to plan for it. Bright lights, crowded spaces, and relentless noise are part of my profession, but they don't have to undo me. I keep sunglasses in my bag for sudden glare. I choose clothing textures I can tolerate for long hours under hot studio lights. I carry discreet noise filters that let me be present in chaotic environments without burning out.

Equally important are my exits — both physical and emotional. I build in quiet time between obligations, even if it's just a five-minute walk outside or a retreat into a quiet corner with my phone silenced. I've learned not to apologize for needing those breaks. They aren't indulgences; they are maintenance, like charging a battery before it dies.

These tools are not extraordinary, and that is the point. They are small, steady habits that keep me aligned in a world that often feels jagged. They remind me that living with autism isn't about erasing difference, but about creating systems that allow difference to thrive.

The truth is, the tools that stick are not just for survival. They are for flourishing. They allow me to show up — for my work, for the people I love, and for myself — not perfectly, but fully. And in that fullness lies the life I once thought was out of reach.

Reflection, Advocacy, and What I Want the World to Know

ON LABELS, IDENTITY, AND THE SPECTRUM

MY VIEWS ON THE TERM AUTISM AND WHAT IT HAS MEANT PERSONALLY AND CULTURALLY

The word *autism* entered my family's life like a key — one that unlocked a door we had been pushing against blindly for years. At first, it was terrifying, a label that seemed heavy with stigma and uncertainty. Over time, though, it became something else: not a sentence, but a signpost. It gave context to my struggles, a shared language for my family and my teachers, and eventually, a way for me to advocate for myself.

But labels, even when useful, are double-edged. The word *autism* explained me, but it never contained me. I've wrestled with the tension between appreciating the clarity it brought and resisting the stereotypes that trailed behind it. Culturally, the term has shifted over the years — from whispers of deficiency to conversations about neurodiversity and strength. Each shift reflects not only how society sees people like me, but also how people like me come to see ourselves.

To this day, I carry mixed feelings. Autism is part of my story, but it is not the whole book. It is the lens through which many see me, but it is not the lens through which I wish to be entirely defined. I am grateful for the label when it opens doors to understanding. I am cautious of it when it threatens to close them.

The Spectrum as a Map, Not a Prison

What has helped me most is reimagining the idea of the spectrum. Too often, people picture a single line: mild at one end, severe at the other. That model flattens real lives into one dimension. I prefer to think of the spectrum as a map — wide, varied, full of regions with their own landscapes. On some days, I inhabit the high ground of resilience, humor, and sharp focus. On other days, I sink into valleys of sensory overload and exhaustion. The map shifts with circumstance, environment, and energy.

Seeing the spectrum as a map means acknowledging possibility. It means recognizing that a diagnosis does not predict the limits of a life, but rather highlights the terrain a person might need to learn to navigate. For me, it has never been about escaping autism, nor about being defined solely by it. It has been about learning the contours of my own map and finding the routes that allow me to move forward.

I do not wear the label as a badge, nor do I deny it. I use it as a compass when I need direction, and I set it aside when I want to simply *be*. Autism is neither a cage nor a crown; it is one feature of my geography. And like any map, its meaning depends on how you travel it.

PARENTING A CHILD ON THE SPECTRUM — ADVICE I GIVE YOUNG PARENTS

CONCRETE, COMPASSIONATE GUIDANCE FOR PARENTS WHO FEEL LOST

When I meet parents who are just beginning their journey with a child on the spectrum, I often see in their eyes the same fear and bewilderment my parents once carried. They ask: *What do we do now? How do we help without hurting? Where is the map?* The truth is, there is no single map. Every child's needs are unique, every family's capacity is different. But there are principles that matter.

First, don't measure your child against other children. Comparison is poison. It robs you of noticing the small victories — the first time your child holds eye contact for three seconds, the first joke they manage to deliver, the first friend they call by name. Those moments may not appear in a baby book, but they are milestones nonetheless. Celebrate them.

Second, structure is not restriction. Children on the spectrum often thrive on routines, not because it limits them, but because it gives them safety from which to grow. Build predictable patterns for meals, bedtimes, transitions. Within those patterns, leave small doors open for flexibility, so they can practice adjusting without drowning in chaos.

Third, remember that love is not only a feeling, it's a practice. Love looks like patience when progress is slow. Love looks like advocacy when systems fail. Love looks like showing up, again and again, even when you are exhausted.

What I Wish My Parents Had Known and What Worked

Looking back, I realize my parents were pioneers without a guidebook. My father's methods were unconventional, sometimes harsh, sometimes brilliant. What I wish they had known was that they didn't have to carry it all alone. Community, therapy, and support groups exist now in ways that were sparse when I was growing up. Parents today should not be afraid to reach out, to admit that this journey is bigger than any one household.

At the same time, many of the things my parents did *did* work. My father's insistence on practicing social skills — even when I resisted — gave me the ability to function in spaces that once terrified me. My mother's quiet patience, her willingness to let me retreat and recharge, gave me the space to survive those lessons. Their balance — one pushing, one protecting — became the foundation I still stand on.

If I could offer young parents one final piece of guidance, it would be this: your child is not broken. They are not waiting to be "fixed." They are waiting to be understood. See their strengths, not just their struggles. Nurture the spark of who they already are, not only the image of who you thought they would be. If you do that, you will give them what my parents, despite their stumbles, ultimately gave me: a life where difference does not mean less, and where love is never in question.

SYSTEMS THAT HELP — SCHOOLS, HEALTHCARE, POLICY

PRACTICAL REFORMS AND RESOURCES THAT WOULD HAVE MADE A DIFFERENCE

When I look back at my early years, I realize how much of my progress depended not on systems, but on the determination of one father who refused to give up. That fact is both inspiring and troubling. It should not take a parent's total sacrifice to make the difference between thriving and floundering. Systems exist for a reason — to give families tools they cannot build alone.

In schools, what would have helped me most was not just a label on a file, but teachers trained to recognize the signs and strategies of autism. A patient teacher who understands sensory overload can transform a classroom into a safer space. A simple accommodation — quieter seating, structured peer support, visual aids — can make the difference between despair and learning. Reform means equipping educators with both resources and empathy, so that no child is left at the mercy of guesswork.

In healthcare, early and accessible interventions matter most. Speech therapy, occupational therapy, counseling — these should not be luxuries rationed by cost or location. Families need systems that recognize the urgency of early years and provide consistent, affordable care. For me, it often felt like my parents had to fight for every session, every evaluation, every ounce of support. Reform means shifting from scarcity to sustainability.

Policy, too, shapes possibility. Families should not face financial ruin for doing what is necessary to support a child with autism. Insurance coverage, workplace flexibility for caregivers, and public investment in neurodiversity education are not extras; they are lifelines. What would have made a difference in my own story is a world where my father did not have to abandon his career to give me a chance. Systems that truly help would give parents the ability to support their children *without losing themselves.*

Where Institutions Still Fail Families Like Mine

Even now, institutions often lag behind the needs of families. Schools may recognize autism on paper but still stigmatize it in practice. Healthcare providers may offer therapies, but access is uneven, especially across income levels or geographic regions. Policy debates often reduce autism to statistics, forgetting that behind every number is a child, a family, a future that hangs in the balance.

Too often, families are left to stitch together their own patchwork of solutions. A supportive teacher here, a kind therapist there, a policy loophole that helps for a time — but no comprehensive net to catch them. The result is exhaustion, isolation, and a sense that survival depends on luck more than fairness.

What families like mine need is not sympathy, but infrastructure. Systems that assume every child deserves a chance. Systems that train teachers, fund therapies, protect parents, and create pathways for autistic individuals not only to survive, but to flourish.

My story is proof of what is possible when one family gives everything. But it should also be a call to build systems that don't demand such extremes. Because every child, regardless of zip code or income or diagnosis, deserves a world ready to meet them where they are — and walk with them into where they can go.

WHEN THE STORY BECOMES PUBLIC — MEDIA, MISUNDERSTANDING, OPPORTUNITY

How Public Narratives Shape Perceptions of Autism

Autism, for much of my life, was a private reality — something navigated within the walls of my home, carried into schools, and wrestled with in silence. But once my story intersected with journalism, I realized that personal experience and public narrative do not always align. Too often, the media frames autism in extremes: the tragic burden or the miraculous savant. These portrayals may attract headlines, but they flatten the reality. Most of us live between those poles — not broken, not genius, but human beings learning to thrive in our own ways.

The narratives people consume matter. They shape how teachers approach a student, how employers judge an applicant, how families feel about their own child's future. When the story is told poorly, it builds barriers. When it is told honestly, it can open doors of empathy and understanding.

The Responsibility of Storytellers and Journalists

As a journalist, I've carried the tension of being both a subject of autism's story and a narrator of it. I know the weight of representation — how one interview, one headline, one sound bite can shape perceptions far beyond the moment. Storytellers hold immense power. We can stigmatize with a careless phrase, or we can dignify by showing complexity.

For me, this responsibility has become personal. I don't just tell other people's stories; I stand as proof of the stakes. I know what it feels like to be misunderstood, and I know the relief of being truly seen. That knowledge pushes me to approach narratives about autism with care. I avoid caricature. I search for nuance. I try to balance challenges with strengths, so that no one walks away thinking autism means only one thing.

The opportunity here is vast. Media can become not just a mirror of society's fears, but a megaphone for possibility. Every article, every broadcast, every documentary can shift the cultural conversation one notch closer to truth. But that requires journalists to resist the easy tropes and commit to depth.

My story is one of many, but if telling it publicly helps even one parent feel less alone, or one young person feel less invisible, then the discomfort of exposure is worth it. Because in the end, the story of autism is not mine alone — it is a collective story, still being written, and how we tell it will determine how we live it.

Made in the USA
Monee, IL
30 September 2025